DIANA
TWENTIETH-CENTURY PRINCESS

DIANA
TWENTIETH-CENTURY PRINCESS

BY PATRICIA REILLY GIFF

Illustrated by Michele Laporte

SCHOLASTIC INC.
New York Toronto London Auckland Sydney

For Regina Hayes
with love

Revised edition reissued 1997

ISBN 0-590-04728-0

12 11 10 9 8 7 6 5   8 9/9 0 1 2 3/0

Printed in the U.S.A.   40

First Scholastic printing, February 1998

CONTENTS

1

The Young Diana

A glass coach drawn by dapple-gray horses waited outside Clarence House. Almost a million people lined the streets. Some of them had been there for days—sleeping on rolled-up blankets, eating from picnic baskets.

At Buckingham Palace, bakers were putting final touches on the 168-pound cake. Forty-nine pounds of white icing decorated the top and sides.

Inside Clarence House, the home of Elizabeth the Queen Mother, the bride was almost ready. The hairdresser had arrived with his bag of ten combs, rollers and brushes, and three hair dryers.

The wedding dress had arrived, too. It was a marvel of ivory silk taffeta with a 25-foot train, the longest in the history of England. Sewn inside was a tiny gold and diamond horseshoe for luck.

The bride was Lady Diana Spencer. She was marrying His Royal Highness, Prince of Wales, Charles Philip Arthur George, the man who would be the next king of England.

Everyone agreed she would be a perfect queen. But to everyone, most of all Diana, it was a surprise.

Most of the time Diana wore jeans, or sweaters and skirts. At age 16, she had left school. Until a few months before the wedding, she had taken care of babies and cleaned people's houses. She had a part-time job as a teacher's assistant.

But Diana was not an ordinary girl. She came from a long line of royals. Henry VII, an English king in the 1400s, had been one of her ancestors. Her father held the title of Viscount (say "Vy-count"). This title is passed down from father to son. It means that he is considered a nobleman.

Diana was also related to eight American presidents. George Washington was one; Ronald Reagan was another.

She was born on July 1, 1961, a lovely baby. Her parents, John Spencer, the Viscount Althorp ("Allthrup"), and his wife, Frances, were disappointed, though. This was their third daughter. They had hoped so much for a son it had taken them a week to decide on her name: Diana Frances.

A year later, Sarah, Jane, and Diana had a baby brother, Charles. Not too long after, Diana's mother fell in love with another man. She left their home and her children behind.

Diana was the child who was most upset by the divorce. "I'll never marry unless I'm really in love," she told a friend years later. "If you're not sure you love someone, you might get divorced. I never want to get divorced."

Diana had always been a sunny child. Now she became sad and sometimes moody. She hated to leave her father alone when she went to visit her mother. When she came home again, she felt sorry about leaving her mother.

Her new nanny, Mary Clark, had worried about

this when she took the job. She remembered hearing that Diana had locked one nanny in the bathroom. She had thrown another nanny's clothes up on the roof. Diana was a neat child, a pretty child, a sweet child, but she had a mind of her own!

After the holidays, when Diana was 11, she returned home after a visit to her mother. She was sad and angry.

It was time to dress for a party given by the queen of England. But Diana refused to go, and even when Mary, the nanny, tried to talk her into it, she shook her head. They had to leave her at home. Once she had made up her mind, it was impossible to change it.

Diana didn't like to think about school, but she loved outdoor sports and dancing. Although she had been forbidden to do it, she loved to climb to the top of the slide, and dive into the deep end of their outdoor pool. She especially enjoyed showing off her beautiful dive in front of company.

Diana loved babies. She practiced by taking care of her little brother Charles. She loved to feed him and play with him. When he outgrew his baby clothes, she used them to dress her teddy bear.

She loved animals, too. At different times she mothered ponies, horses, a cat named Marmalade, and a guinea pig named Peanuts.

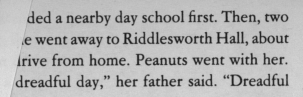 ded a nearby day school first. Then, two
.e went away to Riddlesworth Hall, about
rive from home. Peanuts went with her.
dreadful day," her father said. "Dreadful

Diana felt dreadful, too, at first. She missed being
home, and everything at school seemed new and different. Miss Ridsdale, the headmistress, placed top
priority on happiness. She was strict about some
things, though. Students could have only one piece
of candy a day on weekdays, and when birthdays came,
no presents from home were allowed.

But soon Diana grew used to the sound of the
cowbell that woke them in the morning. She'd dress
in her gray uniform and wait in line to have her hair
braided. Then it was fun to rush to the pet center to
take care of Peanuts.

Quickly she made new friends. Teachers approved
of her. She was neat and careful about her things.
Even though she giggled a lot, she was a good girl
and did what she was told.

When she was 14, it was time for more serious
study. In two years, Diana would have to take her O
Levels. These are tests that each student in England
must pass in every subject in order to continue his or
her education. Then, at age 18, the student must pass
his A Levels to enter a university.

Diana's father enrolled her at West Heath School, a boarding school about 30 miles from London. Again she made friends quickly. She whispered and sneaked chocolates with them after lights out.

She made friends with an old woman who lived nearby, and shopped for her and made her tea. She also helped handicapped children at a nearby shelter when she had time.

Diana was quiet and shy, with a great sense of humor. She was poised. Her manners were beautiful. She loved dancing, especially ballet. "I'm obsessed with ballet," she told her friends later. "I always wanted to be a ballet dancer . . . but I just grew too tall."

She couldn't study, though, or wouldn't study. She used her free time to read romantic novels or to watch television.

At 16, she should have been working on her O Level examinations. Instead of passing a dozen tests, she didn't pass one. She tried again, and failed them all.

There was no chance for her to enter England's university system, or even to graduate from what in America would be called high school.

No one could be sure whether Diana was upset or not. But one friend knew that she kept a scrapbook of famous people who had never finished school.

Diana decided not to stay at West Heath. Instead, she entered a fine finishing school in Switzerland, a school which prepares young women for their life in society and gives lessons in cooking, sewing, and skiing. French was the language spoken every day. Diana couldn't master French and there were only a few other English girls with whom she could speak.

The school was a serious mistake for Diana. She was homesick and miserable. She lasted a few weeks, then flew home. At 16, her education was finished.

She was unprepared for the business world. She had no interest in trying for a secretarial position.

Two things stood out about Diana Spencer though, and she used them both. She had been a neat, organized child, and she loved children.

Not trained to teach, she could still take care of children, and she could clean other people's houses. She enjoyed doing both.

She moved into her mother's house in London, and began to teach dancing to two-year-old children at Miss Vacani's School. At the same time, she herself took lessons.

After one term, Diana found an apartment of her own at 60 Coherne Court in Chelsea. She moved in with two friends. The apartment was near Sloane Square, an area where many of England's well-to-do young people lived. They dressed in skirts and sweat-

ers and wore dainty gold or pearl necklaces—and were called the Sloane Rangers.

By this time, she had had enough of teaching dancing. Instead, she became a baby-sitter for a little American boy who was living with his family in London.

Then she was able to get a position at the Young England Kindergarten. It was perfect for her. She could ride there on her bicycle; she could work with children ages two to five. She was wonderful at helping them with their art projects and listening to their problems. One mother called her "a pied piper with children."

She still thought about being a dancer. She thought about being married, too. Her sister Sarah had been dating Prince Charles. Diana had had a secret crush on him for years, even pinning up a magazine picture of him over her bed.

What would it be like to be married to the future king of England, she wondered to one of her friends.

2

Diana and Charles

Buckingham Palace stands in the heart of London.
Some people call it the home of the greatest soap-
opera family in history.

Those who are interested in this family—and that
includes almost everyone in England—are called royal
watchers. You can see them looking up when they
pass the palace. If a gold flag flutters overhead, they
know the most important member of the family is in
residence. Her name is Elizabeth Alexandra Mary
Windsor, but no one calls her that. In private, her

family calls her Lilibet. To the rest of the world, she is Elizabeth II, queen of Great Britain, Canada, Australia, and 17 other countries. She is head of state of almost 50 more in the Commonwealth.

Great Britain, the heart of the Commonwealth, is a land of castles, many of them said to be haunted, with eerie noises at night, and horseshoes nailed over doorways for luck. Imagine a country with towns named Great Snoring, Mousehole, Catbrain, Affspuddle, and Blubberhouse.

Imagine going into a restaurant and asking for rumplethumps when you want a dish of mashed potatoes, cabbage, and cheese. Perhaps you might enjoy some black pudding, a kind of sausage, or a dollop of clotted cream to put on a scone.

In school, when you open a history book, you have 1,000 years of kings and queens to study. More interesting than reading about them is standing on the very spots where they stood.

From Buckingham Palace it's a short subway ride to the Tower of London. Be glad you weren't around in the days of King Henry VIII. You can touch the stones where two of his six wives were beheaded. You might walk to Winchester Cathedral to see the tomb of the first Queen Elizabeth. Not far away is the tomb of her cousin Mary, Queen of Scots, whom Elizabeth I had beheaded.

There you can see the tomb of Queen Victoria, whose nine children and 49 grandchildren ruled in different countries throughout Europe. Victoria was the great-great-grandmother of Queen Elizabeth II.

English schoolchildren can rattle off the whole line of royalty from the Victorian days. First there was Victoria, they say. Her son was Edward VII, and his son was George V. His son was George VI, and because he had no sons to become king, his daughter, today's Elizabeth II, became queen.

Great Britain is a modern empire, too. It is made up of the countries of England, Scotland, and Wales. London, its most famous city and the capital of England, is one of the great commercial and financial centers of the world. In between its old buildings are sleek, modern ones made of glass and steel, and skyscrapers. London is also known for music, drama, and good books.

Three-quarters of Britain is farmland, with farmers raising enough wheat, potatoes, vegetables, and fruit to feed most of the population. The quiet fields are dotted with sheep and cows, and fishermen take their boats out every day to provide a fresh catch.

Britain is a major industrial nation. It is ranked in the top ten of the world's oil and steel producers. The country earns money from tourism, banking, and insurance, as well.

Laws are made by Parliament, which is made up of the House of Lords and the House of Commons. An elected prime minister is like an American president.

If Great Britain is such a modern country, why is there still a royal family? Why are there palaces with footmen? Why do old customs and ceremonies continue to exist in the same way they did hundreds of years ago? Why is this family paid over twenty million dollars a year?

The answer is partly that it is a tradition. The members of the royal family are similar in a way to movie stars, but more, they seem to belong to all the families in England.

The rest of the world is also interested in this family. Tourists come to see their country, their palaces, and even hope for a quick glimpse of one of the family. These tourists spend a great deal of money while they're there.

The clothes worn by the royal family, their hobbies, their horses, their furniture are all of interest, and help to make people all over the world want to buy English products.

In such a modern country, the queen is a figurehead. This means she has no real power. She is the ruler, but she doesn't make the rules. However, no act of Parliament can become law without her consent. On the other hand, if Parliament asked for her own death warrant, she would have to sign it. But this would never happen in these modern days.

Elizabeth is a wonderful queen, dedicated to duty. Because she is the mother of three princes and one princess, the royal family is sure to continue. Had her oldest child been a girl, she would have been passed over, and the next oldest son would have been king. But since Elizabeth's first child was a boy, he will be king someday. His sons and daughters will be next in line for the throne.

The name of this future king is Charles Philip Arthur George, and he was born on November 14, 1948.

As Charles grew to adulthood, the royal watchers gathered every scrap of information they could about him. His activities made him seem almost a daredevil. He flew his own plane and helicopter. He took parachute lessons and jumped once, but the queen quickly put an end to that. He loved skiing and sailing. He was graduated from the Royal Naval College and had spent time at sea.

Those who knew him felt he was shy and quiet, a loner. In fact, the reason for all the daredevil behavior was probably to make his father approve of him.

His father was strict, almost cruel, given to using harsh language, and had often frightened Charles as a child.

Prince Philip wished his son were tougher, more

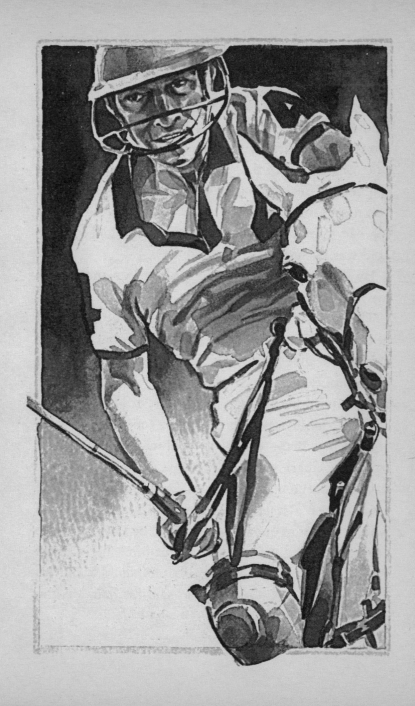

like his younger sister, Anne. But Charles was the queen's favorite. He had a wonderful, warm relationship with her.

Charles held the titles of Duke of Cornwall and Rothesy, and in 1969, when he was 21, his mother crowned him Prince of Wales. This is a traditional title for the heir to the throne, and the ceremony was splendid. There was only one problem. The crown was too heavy for the prince's head. The gold orb on top had to be removed, and a Ping-Pong ball sprayed gold was pasted on instead.

By the time Charles was 32, all of England waited for his marriage.

The woman he would marry had to be approved not only by Elizabeth, but also by Parliament. Neither would ever give approval if the woman were divorced or Catholic. She'd have to be able to have children, and it would be a bonus if she were royal.

The trouble was, there weren't too many women around like that—especially a woman who appealed to Prince Charles.

Charles seemed stuffy and old-fashioned. He wanted an old-fashioned woman. "I wouldn't have a woman libber as one of my friends," he told the press.

And how did women feel about him? He was tall but certainly not handsome. People talked about his "jug-handle" ears. One woman said his hair was too short and greasy. Another was angry when he ignored her at the dinner table to talk with some friends. She left, and wouldn't see him again.

Still, Charles was the most eligible bachelor in England—and probably the entire world. He received 4.3 million dollars each year from rental properties in Cornwall, he had many private investments, and even held the rights to whales that washed up on the beaches in the west. When his mother dies, he will inherit approximately five billion dollars in property, paintings, jewelry, and cash.

Wherever he went, reporters and photographers followed. If he spoke with a woman, the newspapers would announce his engagement. Strangers would swoop up to kiss him, and their faces would appear in magazines.

Everyone wanted to know who would be the woman with whom he'd fall in love. But Charles would say, "Falling madly in love with someone is not necessarily the starting point to getting married. If I'm deciding on whom I want to live with for fifty years—that's the last decision in which I would want my head to be ruled entirely by my heart."

All that would change during the next two years. Prince Charles was beginning to notice Diana.

Of course he had known her for years. His grandmother, Elizabeth the Queen Mother, and Diana's grandmother, Lady Ruth Fermoy, were close friends. They had always hoped he would marry one of the Spencer girls.

He began to date Sarah, Diana's older sister. One day he was invited to Althorp, the Spencer home, for a pheasant shoot. Diana was there.

That day, Charles was delighted with the way she looked up at him from under her eyebrows. Her eyes were a beautiful blue, her skin glowed. She giggled, and played with a small gold *D* necklace, making sure to hide her bitten fingernails. At the same time, she stooped a little, trying to seem smaller than he, although they were both exactly the same height: five feet, ten inches.

Charles was even more entranced with Diana when she taught him to tap-dance a few months later at a weekend party.

But she still seemed young to Charles, very young. It took two years for him to make up his mind.

It didn't take long for the press to find out when he started to send her roses. They knew almost immediately that he had taken her to dinner, and that she had been included in parties he attended.

Reporters began to gather at her apartment. They waited outside the school where she taught part-time. They even followed her in cars, and on foot, to the grocery store, to the Sloane Square shops, to her friends' homes.

Flashbulbs went off in her face. Questions were shouted at her.

Sometimes she escaped out her back door and sped away in her little red car. More than once, she cried. For the first time, she began to realize it might not be so easy to be a princess.

3

The Wedding

In February, five months after they began to date, Prince Charles invited Diana to dinner in his rooms at Buckingham Palace. That night he asked her to marry him.

She said yes immediately.

But the prince asked her to wait. "I wanted to give her time to think about it," he said.

He told her to decide while she was in Australia for three weeks to visit her mother. "Think about whether it will be too awful," he said.

He knew Diana would be living a very different

life. Everything she wore, everything she said in public, everything she did, would be talked about on TV, or written in the newspapers. She would spend her life going from one public event to another, planting trees, dedicating new buildings, schools, and hospitals. State ceremonies would keep her standing for hours on end. Charles had been trained for all that . . . even taking school lessons standing up instead of sitting. It would be all new for her.

Diana didn't need time to think. She was ready.

The queen was delighted. Diana was perfect. She was English, she came from an old family, and she was a member of the same church.

Parliament quickly agreed.

The country went wild. Everyone, it seemed, fell in love with the 19-year-old who someday would be the queen of England.

They admired her beauty and enjoyed her giggles. They were charmed by the way she stopped to talk with people on the streets, and by her closeness with children, and her gentleness with old people.

They couldn't wait for a royal wedding. It would be a party for the entire country.

Elizabeth sent to Garrads, the royal jewelers, and had a tray of beautiful rings sent to the palace. Diana could choose her favorite.

Laughing, she told her friends she had chosen the

largest, the loveliest. The center stone was a huge blue oval, an 18-karat sapphire. It was surrounded by 14 diamonds. It cost the prince more than $60,000.

After all the excitement, their first separation was coming. Prince Charles had promised to make a five-week tour of Australia, New Zealand, Venezuela, and Washington. Diana waved good-bye as the plane took off. Everyone could see she was crying.

"It really was most touching," one of the royal party said, "but she must learn to keep a stiff upper lip."

Diana had to become someone people admired. She had to appear strong, and certainly couldn't cry in public.

So many things had to be learned during the five weeks Prince Charles was away. Diana stopped working at the children's school, and moved into quarters at Buckingham Palace. The Queen Mother, Elizabeth herself, would be her teacher.

Diana had to learn to wear hats as the rest of the royal family did. She had to accept the fact that her friends would curtsey to her, just as she had to curtsey to the queen.

Even though she always had good posture, she was marched up and down the palace ballroom with a sheet trailing behind her. It was good practice. The train she would wear on her wedding day would be heavy, and the aisle at St. Paul's Cathedral was very long.

She had to make time for her royal portrait. The artist painted Diana sitting sideways in a chair, wearing a dark pants suit with an ivory shirt. She was smiling slightly.

Princess Anne, Charles's sister, was doing very little smiling those days. Diana had stolen the limelight. Reporters were no longer as interested in the princess. She had never been popular with the press. In fact, she was so difficult that she was often called "Her Royal Rudeness."

Now, being compared to the beautiful Diana made matters worse. Anne rarely smiled; Diana not only smiled, she blushed and giggled. Diana never spoke sharply to reporters; she confided in them about how happy she was. "With Charles beside me, I can't go wrong," she told them shyly.

All of England was gearing up for the wedding. It would be a breath of fresh air at a time when the economy was poor. Many people were out of work, and British industry was not doing well. They needed something happy to cheer them up.

Weeks before the wedding, window spaces along the route to the church were being sold. And people planned parties of their own with champagne and dancing.

Tailors and seamstresses sewed night and day to get

clothes ready for the members of the wedding and the lucky guests.

The designers chosen by Diana to make her wedding dress bought a special safe for the patterns and fabric. Everyone wanted an advance peek at the gown, but the designers were keeping it secret. Extra button coverings and unnecessary snippets of lace were burned at the end of each day.

Diana hired interior decorators and gardeners for Charles's estate, Highgrove House. After the wedding the royal couple would live there. Diana wanted rich coral pinks, greens, and yellows, instead of the present drab beige.

At the same time, Diana began to realize the queen would have an enormous say in her life. She asked permission for one of her former roommates to be in her wedding party. The queen refused. Diana's five bridesmaids were all to be children, or at least younger than she.

Diana made another request. She wanted to spend the evening before the wedding with her friends. That, too, was refused. The queen told her it would be more proper to have dinner with her mother, then go to bed early.

That night, Diana went to bed to the sound of 12,000 rockets. It was a magnificent display of fireworks. Outside, Prince Charles lighted a bonfire. It was the first in a chain of 101 that would be set on fire across the entire country.

Then at last, it was the day of the wedding. It was a national holiday with no school for the children. Queen Elizabeth wore aqua, Princess Anne wore yellow, and the Queen Mother wore blue.

Never before had so many people watched a wedding. For those who couldn't actually be in London, there was TV. In Canada and the United

States, where the time was six hours behind, people set their alarm clocks for dawn. They rushed to their living rooms in bathrobes to see Lady Diana say, "I will."

As the 11:00 A.M. bells began to peal on July 29, eleven clergymen wearing red, gold, and silver came down the aisle. Five bridesmaids and two page boys followed.

Then, slowly, Diana started down the aisle with her father. He had been sick, and was still shaky. Diana

steadied him. "She was a tower of strength," he said afterward.

She seemed so poised that it was a surprise when she said, "I was so nervous I hardly knew what I was doing."

Trumpets and the cathedral organ provided stirring music, chosen by Charles. "It has to be stirring," he said, "dramatic and noisy, because if you had something quiet, you'd start hearing your ankles cricking."

At the altar, Charles waited. "You look wonderful," he told Diana, as she joined him there.

"Wonderful for you," she whispered.

They said their vows looking solemnly at each other. Charles was as nervous as she. Instead of saying, "All *my* worldly goods with thee I share," he said, "All *thy* worldly goods with thee I share."

Princess Anne loved it. "He meant it," she said.

Diana, too, made one mistake. She said, "I take you, Philip Charles Arthur George," instead of Charles Philip Arthur George.

"She's marrying my father," Prince Andrew teased and handed Charles the ring for Diana. It was made from the last piece of a nugget of gold mined in Wales in 1922. The nugget had provided rings for the queen, the Queen Mother, Princess Margaret, the queen's sister, and Princess Anne.

Then the archbishop of Canterbury announced: "I pronounce that they be man and wife together."

The newlyweds returned to the palace in an open carriage. One thousand doves were released along the way, and showers of roses, rice, and confetti. The frenzied crowds kept shouting, "Lady Di, Lady Di."

Before Charles and Diana left for their honeymoon, they returned to the palace balcony four times to wave to the crowds in the parked square below.

"Kiss, kiss," thousands of voices shouted.

The prince glanced at the queen. When she smiled and nodded a little, he leaned over to kiss the bride.

"None of us will ever forget the atmosphere," he said later. "It was electric, almost unbelievable. . . . I was quite extraordinarily proud to be British."

For Diana, it was the beginning of a new life. It would be completely different from what had been before.

4

New Beginnings

The wedding was over, but no one wanted the party to end. The royal family held a ball that lasted almost all night. Even the queen danced a little jig before she waved good night. And it was almost dawn before the streets cleared as people started for home.

In spite of the huge crowds, it had been a remarkably safe wedding. No one had been hurt. Only one person had been arrested for pickpocketing.

Not everyone was happy, though. "Rock Against Royalty" concerts were held. Here and there, T-shirts were seen that read, WHAT WEDDING? One person wrote to *The Times* newspaper of London. She said she was angry at the showiness and extravagance of the wedding. It was true that the wedding had cost a staggering amount of money. The queen paid for the wedding itself, but the Department of Environment had spent $100,000 to decorate the streets leading to St. Paul's Cathedral and to find a red carpet for the center aisle.

In Parliament, Willie Hamilton reminded people, "If two miners each earn twenty pounds a week, they will have to work fifty years before they will make what we give this young twerp in a year." The twerp, of course, was Prince Charles, and although Charles does not receive an allowance from the government as the rest of the royal family does, his income from the rents in Cornwall and in London are very high. Some members of Parliament feel these rents are unearned.

Most of England was satisfied with the joy of the wedding day, however. The money spent by tourists had been high and had made up for some of the government expenses. Diana and Charles were satisfied, too. They left by train for Broadlands, the estate where the queen had started her own honeymoon.

Two days later, the royal couple arrived at the docks to board the royal yacht *Britannia*.

As it left the harbor, reporters and photographers

tried to follow. This time, they were unsuccessful. Everyone who had anything to do with the honeymoon kept the secret. Frustrated, the press called the *Britannia* "the ghost ship."

Royal watchers were frustrated, too. They didn't want to let the couple go. They wanted to hear more, read more of the fairy tale.

What was it like to be on a ship with a crew of 276 to take care of them? How would it feel to be the only ones in the sparkling swimming pool on deck, to be the only moviegoers in the ship's theater, to have a whole ballroom to themselves?

Everyone wanted to know what the princess would wear on the royal honeymoon. They loved the idea of a young pretty princess who would wear beautiful clothes. She would be a style setter.

For too long there had been little of interest to see in royal clothing. Elizabeth the Queen Mother was elderly and the queen herself was middle-aged. They weren't interested in being fashionable. Charles's sister, Princess Anne, was a no-nonsense young woman who was more interested in horses and dogs than in what she wore.

But now the British had someone to imitate. Diana had visited designers at *Vogue* magazine several times. These designers had talked with her about style. They gave her advice on clothes, and makeup, and hair.

Instead of preppy skirts and sweaters, she had begun to wear romantic dresses. They were silky and flowing, with large, soft collars.

Blonde highlights had been added to her hair. Her new haircut, layered on the sides, was called the Princess Di cut, and hairdressers all over the world were copying it. Even her eyelashes had been dyed to frame her lovely eyes. She added her own invention: a blue pencil line under her lower lids. Everyone was copying that, too.

The morning of her wedding, designers snapped photos of her wedding dress. While everyone else was partying, they stitched cheaper versions of the original. Princess Diana wedding dresses were on sale that afternoon for a small amount of the original cost.

After the wedding day, royal watchers had to wait to see more of Diana. Not until several weeks later did the newlyweds make their first official visit: a three-day tour of Wales.

Parliament and the rest of the royal family were uneasy about the trip. Many of the steel and coal mines had been closed in Wales. People were out of work. Political groups plastered slogans against the royals on walls and buildings. A small bomb was found in one of the areas scheduled for the prince's visit.

As it turned out, there was no need to worry. Diana wore green, red, and white, the colors of the Welsh

flag. She stayed out in the freezing rain, shivering, to greet the crowds. She made sure to keep her gloves off because she knew people wanted to see her rings. In careful Welsh she told them: "How proud I am to be princess of such a wonderful place."

One boy called out to her: "My dad says, 'Give us a kiss.'"

"Well, then, you'd better have one," she said, smiling.

Charles held an umbrella over her head. "Here's the person you've come to see," he said over and over.

It was true. They shouted her name, they called to her. Everyone wanted to touch her. It almost seemed that the Welsh people had fallen in love with Diana. As one English newspaper put it afterwards, Diana had WOWED WALES.

Eleven months later, another crowd lined the streets. This time it was in London, outside St. Mary's Hospital. The news had been passed along that Princess Diana was ready to have her first baby.

It was June 21, 1982. At 9:03 that evening, a baby boy was born. His eyes were a deep blue like his grandmother's, Queen Elizabeth. His hair was blond.

At the hospital, the crowd had swelled. "Charlie! Charlie!" they chanted as they waited for the prince to come outside.

When he finally appeared, they wanted to know the baby's name.

Prince Charles couldn't answer that question. "You'll have to ask my wife," he said. "There's a bit of an argument about it."

Everyone felt Charles wanted to name the baby after his grandfather, King George VI. His widow, Elizabeth the Queen Mother, would have loved it, and Charles had always been close to her. She was the one in the family who loved children, who understood them. She always kept jars of lollipops around for them.

It seemed Diana had the final say, though. One royal watcher said that she was "a woman of decision and strong will, who is likely to have her way on all matters on which she feels strongly."

Someone else went one step further. "Diana is one of the bossiest people they've ever had in the royal family," she said. "Imagine the effect she's going to have on the royal family over the next twenty years."

The final decision was to call the baby William Arthur Philip Louis.

Diana may have had last say on William's name, or Wills, as he was to be called. But she wouldn't be permitted to decide everything. William was now second in line to the throne. This meant that Queen Elizabeth, the prime minister, and even the archbishop of Canterbury would have a huge say in the

school he attended, what he'd study, and even who'd be invited to his christening.

It wasn't long before another announcement was made. In September, 1984, the crowds gathered again at St. Mary's Hospital. Outside the hospital, Prince Charles told the crowd that the new prince was "absolutely marvelous."

This time there wasn't a problem with the name. The baby was christened Henry Charles Albert David. His family would call him Harry.

The new baby was third in line for the throne. His life would be quite different from little Prince William's. Diana said, "My second child will never have quite the same sort of pressure or problems to put up with that poor William must confront all his life."

Harry would have other pressures, though. His older brother would always be more important, would always come first. Harry would even have to walk two steps behind William when he became king.

It didn't take long to see the difference between the two boys. Harry was sweet, easygoing; William was full of mischief. The newspapers reported everything William did.

He pushed a security button, and the police force arrived. He flushed his toys down the toilet, then tried to flush his father's shoes down.

At a birthday party, he threw food around. When he was scolded, he frowned. "Do you know who I am? When I'm king, I'll send my knights after you."

The television cameras zeroed in for his first word in public. It was "yuck." That was a word Diana used often when she was irritated with something: the traffic, the press, even her hairdo.

Both Prince Charles and Princess Diana wanted their children raised gently, without screaming or a great deal of discipline. Charles's own father had always been stern and unbending. He was angry because Charles spent more time with his family than making royal appearances. Because of this, Prince Philip hadn't even come to see baby Harry until five weeks after he was born.

But even the prince seemed to be upset by Prince William's behavior. "He's very destructive," Charles told a friend. "He has to be watched like a horse." Diana laughingly admitted that William was a little pest.

Queen Elizabeth was shocked when she saw the children fight at the dinner table and talk back to their parents. "Get a new nanny," she was supposed to have told Charles. Almost at once, the old nanny was gone. A new, stricter nanny was hired.

It was not easy for Diana to see William being called

"His Royal Naughtiness" in the newspaper. In fact, she was finding out that her new life was more and more difficult.

At one point, she became so sick of the reporters and photographers following her that she refused to look up so they could take her picture. On a skiing trip, she shook her ski poles angrily at the press helicopter that hovered above her head.

It was beginning to seem that, as a style setter, Diana couldn't do anything right. When she added clothes to her wardrobe, the press talked about how extravagant she was. They mentioned that she had spent at least $2500 a week on clothes during the first year of her marriage. Although Diana paid for many of her clothes, she often received discounts. Some stores chose not to cash her checks. Those stores felt the honor of her purchase was important, and that others would buy things that were similar.

If Diana wore the clothing at home, she charged it to an account set up for her by her father. If the clothes were worn to official functions, the bills were sent to Charles's office.

When Diana made a trip to Italy, she wore a gown she had worn earlier. The British press wasn't happy about that, especially when the Italian press wrote about it. She looked like a salesgirl from a department store, they said. Another writer called the dress ugly.

When she wore a white jacket and shirt, fashion designers said she looked like a waiter. In 1987, she was taken off the list of the world's best-dressed women.

Diana was expected to make many appearances, but her speeches were written for her. She wasn't allowed to give interviews. Publicity agents for the royal family wanted everyone to see her beauty. They wanted the world to see her warmth with old people and her love for children.

They were aware that Diana didn't have much education, that she read only romantic novels, that she might not be very intelligent. They didn't want everyone else to know it, too. Unfortunately, the *Daily Express* newspaper conducted a poll which said the people of England felt Diana was the dumbest of the royals.

She had problems with other members of the royal family, too. Even though she had begun to call the queen Lilibet as the rest of the family did, the queen was still distant and formal.

Her friendship with Princess Anne did not grow. Even though Anne had begun to take on more and more work for the Crown, Diana received all the publicity. And when Anne was not invited to be a godparent for either of the royal children, Diana and Anne saw even less of each other.

At home, things weren't as happy as Diana had

hoped they'd be. Because of her appearances, she missed William's first birthday and Harry's first words.

She and Charles were not the same, either. Workers began to hear them arguing. Someone said Diana was a shouter, who screeched. Their arguments became so loud that visitors to the palace were told to ignore the couple if they began to scream at each other.

Then their arguments became public. At a hunting meeting, they embarrassed the other guests by their fighting. And one time Charles gave Diana advice about raising children. Diana told him, "If you know so much, why don't you have the next baby!"

When Diana was late for the annual Service of Remembrance at the Royal Albert Hall, everyone turned to stare. Her face and eyes were red. The newspapers immediately reported that she and Charles had been fighting.

They were beginning to see they had different interests. Charles enjoyed gardening. He was interested in architecture and collected antique toilet seats. Diana, on the other hand, enjoyed laughing, and dancing at discos. Neither of them liked being with the other's friends.

One royal watcher said Charles was incredibly selfish. "He insists on getting his own way and gets bad-tempered and childish," said a friend. "He expects everybody to bow and scrape, and he tries to treat his wife the same way."

Charles began to take long vacations without Diana. He spent weeks fishing in Scotland. Reporters began to wonder about divorce.

Diana was learning that being married to a prince didn't mean she was happy all the time. It didn't mean that she could do what she wanted. It certainly didn't mean she was living in a fairy tale.

5

The Working Princess

It was time for some changes in Diana's life.

As Prince Charles had told one group, the monarchy has no power. Parliament makes the laws. The queen herself acts only as an advisor, to give encouragement or warnings. All the rest of the family has is influence.

Diana, because of her beauty, her warmth, and her love of children, had tremendous influence with the British people. She began to use it.

In Washington, D.C., Great Britain held an exhibit called "The Treasure Houses of Britain." It was a collection of paintings, drawings, and books. Charles and

Diana traveled to the United States to help make people aware of the exhibit. Because they went to see it, so did crowds of Americans.

At the same time, Diana visited a J.C. Penney's department store in a Virginia mall. The Penney's chain was selling 50 million dollars' worth of clothing made in England, and her visit would certainly help sales.

For her public appearances, Diana wore clothes that were made only in Great Britain. When the British saw her on TV, they knew they could find her clothes in local stores. People from other countries also knew that what she wore was British. They began to order from British designers. Diana became a walking ad for her country. She was called the fairy godmother of British fashion.

As she became a working princess, her style began to change. The soft, romantic look disappeared. *The New York Times* wrote that the suits and dresses she wore could be worn by successful businesswomen anywhere in the world. She was back on the list of the world's best-dressed women.

Diana's wardrobe would have been envied by any woman. It is thought that she owned about 100 evening gowns, 80 suits, and so many skirts, blouses, and dresses it was hard to count.

She had racks of shoes, many of them flats. She wore high heels only when Charles wasn't around. Because she was his height, 5 feet 10 inches, and perhaps even a speck taller, she was careful not to look as if she was towering above him.

Diana never wore hats before she was married, but it is a rule that the women of the royal family always wear them to formal daytime events. She fell in love with hats when she started to wear them. Soon she had more than 100. Sometimes it took four fittings before she was satisfied with the way they looked.

Two full-time dressers helped the princess. What Diana wore had to be planned weeks in advance. Her dressers made a list of when she wore it, and what the occasion was. As she took off a dress, they always went over it to see if it needed to be mended or cleaned. Everything was hung on padded satin hangers inside covers with her initials.

When she traveled, the clothes were packed in giant aluminum cases, still on the hangers. On one trip to Australia, reporters said that 90 cases were brought, but usually she needed about 20.

The princess worried about all the talk of her wardrobe. She told people she really needed what she had, and that she wore the same clothes many times. When she traveled, she explained, she had to change as many as four times a day. On one trip, she went from a desert day trip to an evening ball.

One event seemed to have changed Diana's life. It

happened during a skiing trip in Switzerland.

Not too long before, Charles's brother Andrew had married Sarah Ferguson. Fergie, as she is called, was fun—loud and jolly. For a time, she and Diana spent a great amount of time together, much of it drinking, staying out at night, enjoying discos.

Then came the skiing party in Klosters, Switzerland. An avalanche swept down the mountain. It killed one of Charles's and Diana's close friends, and seriously injured another.

The tragedy had a tremendous impact on Diana. She realized she wanted to spend her life differently. Parties and staying out late were not important to her. It was the end of her close friendship with Fergie, and the beginning of a very serious time of working for the monarchy.

Diana became the president of 27 charities. Her interest in ballet continued. When she attended a program, the company was sure to raise at least $250,000.

Three major issues became important to her: drugs, AIDS, and marriage problems. And of course, anything to do with children was sure to get her attention.

Royalty, before Diana, seemed part of the past. But Diana was a woman who mixed tradition with new things. Her problems with her family and children helped other people feel better about their own problems. They looked at the way she managed her life, and

tried to manage theirs in a similar way.

For example, at the end of a sports day, eight-year-old William refused to leave with Diana. She followed him out to the field and gave him a quick smack. Other mothers knew that her children were the most important part of Diana's life. They were relieved to see that sometimes she was angry the way any other mother might be.

For a twentieth-century princess, it seemed ridiculous that she couldn't speak in public. There were so many things about which she was beginning to feel strongly.

Diana arranged to take speech lessons. She began to make speeches about her causes. They were major talks well thought out, sincere—talks which she wrote herself.

She was the first one of the royal family to shake hands with a patient who had AIDS. She wanted to let the world know this wasn't a dangerous thing to do. She knew it was important to show the need for sympathy, warmth, and help to people who have this disease. One reporter said, "Shaking hands with an AIDS patient is the most important thing a royal has done in 200 years."

One of her causes was RELATE. This is a group that helps people who have problems in their marriages. She was there often, working. The chairman said, "The biggest compliment I can give is that within a few minutes we had forgotten who she was."

Diana began each day by checking a small typed card that listed her appointments. In her desk was a personal diary. It was made of blue leather with her coat of arms embossed on the front. It held all the appointments she had that no one else had to know about: visits with friends, family outings, quick trips to department stores before they opened for business.

Her diary was even more important than a date book that reminded her of plans she had made. It also contained her thoughts and feelings. Everyone in the royal family has a diary like this. Once a year they are taken to Windsor Castle and stored for the future.

Diana worked out almost every day, playing tennis or taking a quick trip to Buckingham Palace for a swim. It was important for her to stay slim—not only for herself, but also for the British clothes she helped advertise by wearing them.

After her workout, her hairdresser was home waiting for her. Next, she had breakfast, and chose what the menus might be for the rest of the week.

Sometimes she was the hostess for a charity lunch; often she visited children's schools and hospitals. If she had a free night, she loved the movies and the ballet.

Diana tried to arrange her schedule so she could spend time with William and Harry. When they

attended boarding school, the weekends they had at home were precious to her. She took them to sporting events, especially the polo games in which Prince Charles played.

But Diana's relationship with Charles was becoming worse. At one of his games, she perched on his Astin Martin car. In front of photographers he embarrassed her by demanding that she get off. "You'll dent the bodywork," he said.

In other photographs, the world could see how unhappy they were. Charles seemed cold and aloof. Diana looked lonely and sad. She developed some eating problems.

By December 1992, the British Prime Minister announced that Charles and Diana had separated. Sadly, they were divorced on August 28, 1996. Later Diana would say, "I desperately loved my husband."

The title Her Royal Highness was taken from her. Instead, she said, "I'd like to be a queen in people's hearts."

6

"Goodbye, England's Rose"

It was close to midnight on Saturday, August 30, 1997. After dinner at a hotel in Paris, France, Princess Diana entered a car with a friend to drive to a private home. The car, chased by seven photographers, traveled along the Cours Albert, a road that ran along the River Seine. As the car sped into a tunnel, it hit a concrete pillar and smashed into a wall.

Diana was rushed to the hospital, where she died early the next morning.

For several days, Diana's casket lay in the chapel at St. James Palace in London. People stood in line for up to eleven hours to sign books with their thoughts and feelings about Diana. They left sad notes and bouquets of flowers on the ground. In other countries flowers were left at the British Embassy. It seemed that the whole world was mourning for this modern-day princess.

On September 6, 1997, all of England came to a standstill. In hushed silence, nearly a million mourners lined the streets, fifty deep in spots, to say goodbye. Throughout the world, people gathered around their television sets. The funeral was broadcast live in forty-four languages.

Inside Westminster Abbey, the ancient cathedral where kings and queens have been crowned for a thousand years, two thousand people waited. Among them were 500 people, many of them handicapped, who represented Diana's favorite charities.

The cathedral bell, muffled by leather around its clapper, rang once every minute as the funeral procession slowly made its way along a three-and-a-half-mile route. The casket was pulled by six horses and surrounded by Welsh guards in red coats. It was draped with the royal standard and covered with flowers. Tucked in a bouquet was an envelope marked "Mummy" in Harry's handwriting.

Just behind the casket, William and Harry walked with their father, Prince Charles; their grandfather,

Prince Philip; and Diana's brother, Charles.

The service began at 11:00 as eight guards carried Diana's casket into the abbey. The sound of Bach's music soared through the cathedral. During the service, Diana's friend Elton John sang new lyrics to his song, "Candle in the Wind," which began, "Goodbye, England's Rose."

Diana's sisters read poetry, and her brother spoke of his big sister, the princess who had become the world's most photographed woman. "She was not a saint but a human being," he told them, with a "laugh that bent her double.

"She would want us today to pledge ourselves to protecting her beloved boys," he said, "and I do this here, Diana, on your behalf."

He reminded the world of Diana's work with the homeless, the lepers, and her fight against the random destruction caused by land mines.

Mourners remembered her recent trip to Bosnia to call attention to the 26,000 people a year who were hurt or killed by land mines. "Someone's got to do something," she had said.

People remembered, too, that she had supported Mother Teresa's Missionaries. Sadly, Mother Teresa died the day before Diana's funeral. They remembered her work for the Red Cross. They thought about the poor babies she had cuddled and the AIDS victims she had hugged. "Whoever is in distress can call on me," she had said. "I will come running wherever they are. It is my destiny."

After the ceremony, the hearse moved through the streets of London on a 77-mile trip to Althorp, where she was buried on an island in a small lake on her family's estate. Along the way, sobbing people gently tossed flowers until the car was blanketed with them.

They spoke of their love for Diana. "She always tried to make everybody feel the same," said one woman.

A fifteen-year-old boy said, "She was the princess of our generation."

Bill Clinton, the president of the United States, said that she had "shown us what it is to live a life of meaning through concern for others."

Perhaps an English nurse said best what most people were thinking. "She was a queen for all of us, rich or poor. She was a special star who lit the sky."